T0149271

Meet
THE
Cousins

Gloreen Hephizibah Burke

authorHOUSE®

AuthorHouse™
1663 Liberty Drive
Bloomington, IN 47403
www.authorhouse.com
Phone: 1 (800) 839-8640

Published by AuthorHouse 04/27/2018

ISBN: 978-1-5462-3785-3 (sc)
ISBN: 978-1-5462-3784-6 (e)

Library of Congress Control Number: 2018904561

Print information available on the last page.

For the millions of people who suffer from Depression.

Acknowledgment

I would like to say a warm thank you to my Publishing Service Associate Ms. Rema Araneta for the wonderful work she has done in designing and putting the book together and to my Publishing Consultant Ms. Kaye Neilson who has taken the time to review all the materials for my book and making sure everything is ok. I couldn't have done it without the help of the both of you.

Dedication

I would like to Dedicate this story to Xaviella and Santana, my three nieces Teanna, Caroline and Cailynn. To all the many Brave and Courageous Men and Women, Soldiers, Police Officers, Fire Fighters, Teachers, Paramedics and Doctors, as well as the many every day Local Heroes whom has given their Lives in the line of Duty in order to save the lives of others and to let their families and friends know that we Truly and Sincerely do Appreciate their Courage as well as the Effort they show as they've work really hard to make the world a better place by doing their best to keep it safe for the rest of us that remains living in it.

May God comforts the Hearts of every Parents' every Wives and Husbands, Every Child, Every Sisters and Brothers, Close friends, Aunts and Uncles who have lost a love one or a Friend to war or has lost their lives in the line of Duty whatever that duty may be.

Let us therefore strive to instil Peace and Harmony for the future Generation to come as violence is not the answer. War and crimes cut lives short and rob innocent infants and children of the opportunity to make it to Adulthood. War and Violence numbs the Heart and prevents the soul from reaching its full spiritual height.

Let us do our part by trying our best to keep the peace.

The Cousins consists of two set of sisters and one cousin. They are all related, Xaviella and Santana are sisters living in Germany. Caroline and Cailynn also two sisters and cousins of Xaviella, Teanna and Santana. Teanna lives in Guelph Ontario. Caroline and Cailynn lives in Brampton Ontario.

Xaviella

Age: 26
Occupation: Doctor
Residence: Germany
Hobbies: Drawing, Dancing, Reading, Traveling, Swimming, Fashion Designing & Shopping

Young beautiful and sexy, highly energetic sports crazy; this young beauty's ambition is to pursue a career in medicine as a Neuro-Surgeon when she grows up. She plays Soccer, Field Hockey, Volley Ball, Does Track and Field and lead her class to a fifth place win in a dance competition against twenty-five other dance groups.

Xaviella is also the Illustrator of several children books. She enjoy playing her Flute and giving dance lessons to her friends and cousins. She's a great cook

Santana

Age:24
Occupation: Pilot/Model
Residence: Germany
Hobbies: Reading, Shopping, Traveling & Hanging out with her friends
Tall elegant and beautiful Santana caught the attention of others everywhere she goes.
She was a model and wishes to be a Pilot when she gets older; she is the Co-Author of a children book title The Magic Cookie. Santana plays the Clarinet and enjoy swimming.

Caroline

Age: 23
Occupation: Squat Police Officer
Residence: Canada
Hobbies: Dancing, Shopping, Badminton, & Reading
Tall petite, sassy, and beautiful this stunning beauty dream of becoming a Police Officer. She loves Dogs and Cats and when she is not busy strolling in the park she can be found watching TV. Caroline plays the Drum and is a member of the Bucket Drumming Team.

Teanna

Age 25
Occupation; News Reporter/Biologist
Residence: Canada
Hobbies: Reading, Scuba Diving, skiing & traveling
Brash and Sassy this athletic Beauty wishes to become a Travel
Journalist for the news. She plays Baseball and is a member
of several Junior Baseball team. Whenever you missed her at
home she is busy teaching younger children to ski. Teanna enjoys
swimming with the dolphins off the coast of Mexico. She loves
to bake and she love her food. She enjoys helping children in
distress and has a passion for rescuing animals. Her favourite
pets are Dogs and Cats.

Cailynn

Age:21
Occupation: Teacher
Residence: Canada
Hobbies; Swimming, Watching TV, Travelling & Hanging out with her Cousins and Friends. Energetic, Feisty, young and Beautiful Cailynn takes no crap from others. She has a passion for Barbie's, and for building things. Spending quality time with her Cousins is her favourite pass time and she has a passion for board games.

Chapter 1

"Now that we've met The Cousins, here's their story"

It all started at a very tender age when these five cousins made a pack with each other that no matter where they go and no matter what they do they'll remain best friends for the rest of their lives. It's very plain to see the reason why, as they are only years apart.

Though they reside in different countries and cities they always find time to chat with each other.

When Xaviella and Santana migrated from Canada back to Germany six years ago Teanna was very sad. Not only did she miss her cousins they were her closest friends.

She spent her time going to school and passes her summer playing baseball, going to her Grandparent's cottage on the weekends and when she's in need of new adventure she would fly to Mexico with her Grandma where she enjoys scuba diving and swimming with the Dolphins.

Caroline and Cailynn has migrated from Canada to Jamaica with their father Ruddy in honour of meeting their great grandmother and their grandfather not to mention a long generation of cousins, as well as their grand aunts and grand uncles. They fell in love with the Islands so much they requested to remain living on the Island for a while.

As not to disappoint them their dad grant their wishes and so they've ended up staying on the Island of Jamaica for two glorious years. Once more Teanna were sad as not just two but four of favourite cousins had move away leaving her behind.

After what seems like an eternity the five cousins were re-united once more. They were flabbergasted to see each other and so on weekends they would all get together and have the time of their life taking long walk in the park, going to the movie, and going to see each other at play when they perform with their favourite team by playing the sports they so love to play.

Time has come for the cousins to be separated once more. Teanna moved away from Brampton and Xaviella and Santana moved to Munich Germany leaving Caroline and Cailynn in Brampton. Thank God for Internet and MSN. Months went by and not a single word was exchanged between these five cousins. The reason being Xaviella and Santana have MSN, but the other girls didn't have MSN.

After speaking on the telephone a couple of times Teanna, Carolynn and Cailynn has decided it's too costly to speak on the phone and so they've decided to make an email account so they could all speak to each other. They were over joy when they received each other's email information and the endless hours of communication began.

Caroline and Cailynn were over joy as they walk to the beach at the foot of the hill. In two days they'll be returning to Canada. Their time on the Island has come to an end, and so they were looking forward to see Teanna, their Aunts, their Grandma along with their neighbourhood friends.

Teanna was over joy when her mom told her that in two days her cousins will be returning from the Island.

"Oh my gosh!" I will get to celebrate Cailynn's birthday with her." She said to her mom.

"Isn't that great?" Her mom replied.

What Teanna didn't know was that Caroline and Cailynn will be attending the same school as her a week after landing in Canada. Hearing this has left her speechless. News reached Xaviella and Santana in Germany of the return of their cousins from the Island.

A few days after their arrival Carolynn, Teanna and Cailynn video call Santana and Xaviella in Germany. They spoke for hours.

Four months later Santana and Xaviella landed at Pearson International Airport in Canada where they join their family and friends for the celebration of Cailynn's seventh-birthday.

Seven Years Later

Today is the happiest day of the Cousins life. It's Graduation day. Teanna, Caroline and Cailynn is graduating from St. Barbara University and Santana and Xaviella graduating from University of Metatron Le'Deleon. They're all on the Honour roll.

The Cousins will never forget their High school years and how they has laboured endlessly. There were times when they thought they would die from exhaustion as they rushed from work to school. Their devotion has paid off when they graduate from High School with Honours and venture off to University.

Now years later they are once more crowned with Honours as they get ready to say goodbye to Teachers and Friends they've made throughout their time in University. Now they're all excited and looking forward to taking on the Real World by putting their Masters and Bachelor's degrees to good use as they work hard to do their part in life.

The parents of the five cousins were over joy to see their baby's all grown up and blossom into beautiful young Ladies that are now venturing out into the world with dignity and honour in pursuing their careers. Graduation ceremony for Santana and Xaviella was held at the

Grand Royal Hotel, while the other three Cousins ceremony was being held at the Lomond International Center.

Teanna, Cailynn and Caroline met at Xaviella and Santana's house where they all got dress and were picked up by two Limousines. How exquisitely stunning they looked.

They hugged each other for a very long time as they wish each other luck.

Santana was dress in a blue Silk gown with lots of sequence, Diamond necklace with matching earrings and bracelet; a pair of blue and silver high heels with lots of diamond looking sequence to match her dress. She was beguilingly beautiful.

Xaviella wore a elegant Peach gown with silver trimmings along the neck, a pair of silver high heels, a white and yellow Gold chain with her name on the pendant with matching earrings and bracelet. She was elegant as well as beautiful.

Cailynn went all out in a Turquoise gown, Pearl Necklace with matching earrings and a pair of white high heels and matching purse. She was breath taken beautiful.

Teanna wore a White gown, Silver necklace with matching Earrings and bracelet and a pair of white high heels. She too was exquisitely beautiful.

Caroline wore a red satin gown with a golden leaf necklace with matching earrings and bracelet with a pair of golden high heels. She was Gorgeous.

Late into the night when the Cousins finished partying with their classmates and friends they rang each other and plan to meet at the Sheraton Hotel, where they'll spend the night together with some of their closest friends.

They all had separate rooms but Xaviella's room was the main room for hanging out before they venture out and retire to their separate rooms. In each room were baskets with variety of fruits, Champagne and Caviar. Yet they took the time to order Pizza, with chicken wings and lots of garlic bread. They ate and talk way into the early morn before they've decided to call it quit and make use of their rooms.

The Cousins woke up the next morning with a terrible hangover. Head pounding and feeling somewhat groggy the girls call room service and request to have their breakfast brought up to their rooms. After eating they were once again energized and ready to go.

One hour later they all meet in the Hotel lobby where they went shopping for clothing, make-up and fragrance in several of the stores located throughout the Hotel lobby taking endless photos as they go along.

Before returning to their rooms the Cousins' made one final stop in the Restaurant and have coffee, cream cheese with bagel, croissants and cheese cake. How quickly the time has past. It was time to check out and return home.

In the land of Chemsie war broke out between the Wasabi Tribe and the Joachite Rebels. The villages are in chaos as food and water supply ran low. Xaviella was at home sitting in her living room. Turning on the Television she caught sight of the war that's going on in Chemsie

'O my God!' this is terrible she said.

Immediately she calls Teanna and informs her of the fighting that's going on in Chemsie.

"Are you serious?" The Wasabi's and the Joachite's is at war? These are the two most feared groups in Chemsie.

"Yes! I just saw it on the news. This is your chance for a great story.

"You are absolutely right, but I need to alert my Boss, and I don't know how quickly I can get a flight, or if my company will allow me to go.

"Give me a few minutes. I will call you back."

"Ok"

At the Algoria Head Quarter Santana was getting ready to go on a test flight. She picked up her helmet and her glasses.

She was about to walk out the door when her cell phone rang.

Sergeant Ambria signal to Santana telling her it's time to go. She answer her phone quickly.

Hey sis just want to tell you that war broke out in Chemsie. The Joachite and the Wasabi's are fighting against each other.

"Oh and Teanna need to get there ASAP, "She would like to cover this story.

"Are you serious?" Santana said sarcastically.

"Are who serious?" Sergeant Ambria asks.

"My sister and my Cousin.

"What have they done now?'

My sister just calls me telling me about the war that broke out in Chemsie, and that my Cousin Teanna needs to get there ASAP to cover the story.

"And what do they expect you to do about it?"

"I don't know!" Fly her there I suppose?

"Now you've lost me," Replied Sergeant Ambria.

"Do you have your own private jet?"

"No!"

"Then how are you supposed to fly your Cousin to Chemsie?"

Tapping her cell phone Santana think the unthinkable. Smiling mischievously she said…

"I think it can be arranged." "You don't mind helping me do you partner?

"Helping you to do what?" Replied Sergeant Ambria.

Before taking off Santana informs Xaviella that she's going test flying right now, and that she'll work on something. Talk to you later. Love you Sis.

Xaviella text Teanna and tell her what Santana said. She then text Caroline and Cailynn also telling them what she saw on the news.

"Don't you just love flying this baby?" Santana ask Sergeant Ambria as they came out a double loop.

"This is what I live for." He replied.

"So you'll help me then?"

"That depends!"

I'm seriously thinking of flying Teanna to Chemsie in one of this baby."

"Are you out of your mind?" "There's no way Head Quarter is going to let you do that."

"You always wanted to spy on Chemsie?"

"You god damn right I do."

"So now is your chance Sergeant."

Chapter 2

We can't just take a One Hundred and twenty four million dollar F-16 fighter jet and fly off without Head Quarter or Lieutenant Donavan's permission.

"That's why we are going to speak to Lieutenant Donavan as soon as we get back.

Sergeant Ambria was about to answer Santana when ….

Mayday mayday, alpha whiskey can you read me?

"Alpha Romeo I read you."

"Return to base immediately." Do you read me?"

"Is there a problem Sir?"

"We've just receive words that the Wasabi's and the Joachite's are at war in Chemise

"We need to send a group of Soldiers there for peace keeping."

"No problem Sir," We'll return to base immediately—Roger out.

"Did I just hear correctly?" Lieutenant Donavan is sending a group of Soldiers to Chemsie for peace keeping?

"You got it partner. I guess your Cousin will get to cover the story after all."

"I guess!" But how do I convince the Lieutenant to let her go along with the crew?

"Just hope and pray that you are going." As long as you are going it won't be difficult to convince him.

Caroline was recruiting a group of Squat officers, briefing them one last time before sending them out to the Ballantine's High School where a class room full of Students are being held hostage. Outside the recruiting room a group of officers could be heard discussing the breaking news on the Chemsie war.

Within minutes the meeting was adjourn. She wishes her team good luck and walk over to a small group of officers and inquire on the status of the Chemsie war.

Everywhere people gossip about the war between the Rebel's and the Wasabi's as fear grips the people knowing, should the Joachites' gain the upper hand over the Wasabis', this could be an invitation for the other neighbouring countries to join in this battle.

The Tahuri Rebels in neighbouring Am Sie along with the Malkerbi Rebels of Hap See not to mention the Chiacah Tribe of Gigota. For years these Tribes and Rebels fought against each other. These Countries have been fighting for century.

"Should we be concern?" Knowing this is no fight of ours?" Caroline ask.

"True this is no fight of ours Constable." However, should the neighbouring countries joins in this fight it's gruesome for all of us; as we'll all be affected to a degree; state Officer Bartley.

"I guess you're right Officer Bartley, but personally, I'm not concern she said before strolling back to her office.

Before sitting at her desk Caroline notice a blink on the computer screen indicating she's got messages. Clicking on the icon her messages pop up.

Hello Caroline this is Xaviella just want to let you know that war broke out in Chemsie and Santana and Teanna is getting ready to fly there. Santana for peace keeping and this is a golden opportunity for Teanna as a reporter to cover this story.

"Do you think they could use our help as well?" Me being a Doctor, and with you being a Police Officer you too can help in keeping the peace and Cailynn can teach the children and find ways to keep them happy. I know it's a war zone but hey we can try and do something for the kids and the innocent families that are paying daily with their lives. Caroline smile and reach for the phone. She hit the speed dial button. On the third ring Xaviella pick up.

"Are you out of your freaking mind Cousin?

"Not at all?"

"Then why do you want us to go to a war zone in Chemsie, a country we hardly know?"

"I just thought we could help the Villagers that's all." And with Santana and Teanna being there, I figure we could keep them sane by showing up.

"Am I to understand that you just want us to leave our jobs here and head off to a country at war?"

"You got it!" Come on—the people could all benefit from our line of work. I can care for the sick and wounded, Teanna Reporting the news so others will know what's going on; you and Santana will be helping to keep the peace while Caitlynn can volunteer to teach the children as a way of cheering them up. You know how well she is with playing games.

"Ok! Ok I understand but even during war life goes on."

"And during war Doctors are needed." As we all know the Wasabi Tribe are poor; fighting always for the betterment of their people, whereas the Joachite Rebels are using up the resources of the Country to fuel their greed for power.

"So, what say you?" Would you like to lend a helping hand?

"Let me think about it Cuz and get back to you later."

"Thanks." Bye Cuz.

Caroline wait? When you have some time can you talk to Cailynn about what we just discuss and tell her to call me?

"Will do!" Bye

Teanna ran through her list one last time making sure she have all the things she need.

She was overly excited to be covering this story, but she was even more excited to be flying in a One Hundred and Twenty-Four Million Dollar F16 fighter jet being fly by Santana her Cousin.

They will be flying with twenty other top-notch fighter Pilots as well. Lieutenant Donavan has agreed after several hours of debating to allow Teanna to fly with his team.

With her equipment's in place Teanna places her cameras and her bag in her car.

Chapter 3

The weather was beautiful and so Teanna puts down the roof of her red Camaro convertible and put on her dark glasses. One hour and twenty five minutes later she pulls up in the parking lot of the Algoria Headquarters' Army Base

Cailynn was in the shower when she heard the phone ringing. Quickly she steps from the shower and ran to the phone. Water dripping everywhere.

"Hello!"

"Cailynn it's me Caroline."

"What do you want?" Aren't you supposed to be on a school premises somewhere trying to free the classroom of Students being held hostage?

"I've already recruit my team and sent them out. I don't go to the scenes of the crime. I brief the team that's responding to the crisis before they go out.

"Yes!" How easy I forget.

"So! what's up?"

Did you hear about the war that's going on in Chemsie?

"Yes, and I think it's awful."

"That's why I'm calling."

"What does Chemsie's war got to do with me?"

Caroline pause for a while then said—Teanna and Santana is on their way there right now as we speak

"Tell me you're joking?"

"No I'm not."

"Ok"

I spoke to Xaviella earlier and she thinks it would be great for us to go as well.

"Me!" Us going to a war zone?"

"Count me out."

"But you didn't let me finish."

"Make it quick so I can return to the shower."

As you know the Wasabi Tribe are very poor and they are fighting for the good of their people, for better housing as well Medicine, Education and more food supplies for the people of the Village; Whereas the Joachite Rebels are fighting for power and using all the funds and resources to fuel their greed for constant dominance.

"And what does that have to do with me?"

With Xaviella being a Doctor, she can attend to the medical need of the people in the village. I can help with peace keeping and you can keep the children's' spirit alive by teaching them.

"Sorry I have no time for this."

"Really Cailynn? Think about it and let me know, Xaviella needs an answer tonight"

"Hmm now can I go and finish shower'?"

'Yes. Love you sis. Bye

It's been a week since Santana and Teanna flew to Chemise with a group of soldiers in honour of keeping the peace, and the Cousins left behind has no news as to their safety or their where about. Xaviella was worried and so she sent Teanna and Santana a text.

"Hey guys it's me just want to know how you guys are doing. I hope that you're both safe. Love you guys. Xavie.

She waits for a reply, but nothing. Half an hour later she got an answer. It was from Teanna.

Santana's Team is doing great. It's extremely hot and chaotic here. People are dying all around us. I'm excited but I'm also scared, be sure to watch the 8: 00 O'clock news as I'll be reporting then.

"Love you and say hi to Cailynn and Caroline. Teanna.

Immediately Xaviella text Caroline and Cailynn, telling them to watch the 8:00 O'clock News on KGB news station. Two minutes after sending the text Caroline reply.

"Cailynn and I are coming over; I'm on my way to pick her up now. See you soon.

Love Caroline.

Xaviella put away a stock of Patient's file she was reading through and went and take a shower. Fifteen minutes later she emerges from the bathroom in her robe with a towel on her head. Picking up the phone she scrolls through the yellow pages for the Mandarins telephone number. She orders sweet and sour chicken wings, Beef fried rice, Seafood with almonds and cashews, three slices of cheese cake and chicken chow Mein.

Cailyn put on her mascara and take one last look at herself in the mirror. Feeling pleased with herself she calls Caroline to see how far she was.

I'll be there in five minutes so please go outside so I won't have to ring the bell.

"Yes mam" I'll go outside.

The Cousins are all living twenty to twenty-five minutes' drive apart. Caroline picked up Cailyn and they were now on their way to Xaviella's house.

Santana, Sergeant Ambrio and three other team members stayed close by as Teanna prepared to report the news back to KGB News Station. She check her micro phone one last time to make sure the connection is clear.

She also checks her footage from the videos she shoots earlier. Everything was perfect.

She was good to go. Ten minutes later she was being connected to KGB News Station.

This is Teanna Lisk reporting from the Village of Malvina in Chemsie. The Leader of the Joachite's Rebels has taken several women and children as hostages from the village of Malvina in hopes that the Wasabi's Gorilla radicals will surrender.

The Joachite Leader states that should the Wasabi Gorillas fail to surrender, the women and children which are being taken hostage will never see their village or their families again. Food and water supplies are running low and the people of the Village are in need of medical and personal supplies as well as Medical care.

It's not looking good for the families with children as well as the Elderly of this poor and impoverish community; they are desperately in need of help. Early this morning ten people were killed four of which being children. I'll keep you up-dated on the status of what's going on.

This is Teanna reporting for the KGB News in Chemsie. Before signing off she send her love to her Cousins.

Hearing such devastating new Xaviella placed the box of food she was eating on the table and face Caroline and Cailyn. They stared at each other in silence. Finally, Cailynn spoke.

`How can they do such thing to those poor people? ``Especially to the women and children?``

`Simple!' Replied Caroline.

They are nothing but a bunch of heartless bastards, she said angrily.

Cutting in xaviella ask them both if they had considered her proposal.

Chapter 4

"I was having second thoughts," Said Caroline.

"Me too!" Chide Cailynn.' But after seeing that horrible footage how can we not go?

"I'm glad you two have come to your senses." Replied Xaviella as she gave them both a hug. "I'll make arrangements with Dr. Shaquille my assistant and Co-Partner. He'll cover for me at the Hospital while I'm away.

"Also I need his help in putting some medical supplies together for our journey.'

Cailynn dial Santana's cell phone number. She was ecstatic to hear her voice on the other end of the line. Santana told her that Teanna was sitting beside her. The girls went wild as they took the time to congratulate Teanna on a job well done. They all converse for a very long time.

Tall handsome and savvy Dr: Shaquille is a very successful and respected intelligent person in his community and at work. He and Dr. Xaviella are the top two Neuro Surgeons at the Sandolphan Hospital. He has big dreams for himself as he and Dr. Xaviella discuss daily of one day building their own Hospital and Research Centre where they'll both research and developed drugs that will cure Epilepsy, Alzheimer and other brain and nerves related illness, as well as healing Manic Depression.

On the 5th day of August 1981 Dr. Shaquille graduated from the La Sivien Medical University with his Bachelor Degree in Neuro Science. It was during his study at the University he met his lovely wife Olivia who at the time was also a student at the University studying Psychology. Their friendship and their love blossom and one year later they got married.

Sergeant Ambria has taken the time to contact Dr. Xaviella the minute he was informed by Santana, that Xaviella and her team is putting together a supply of Medication, food, Personal hygiene items, Blankets and clean drinking water for the people of the Malvina Village. He was also touched to learn that Cailynn and Caroline was accompanying her also, to help out the people of the village.

To ensure that the relief supplies get to Chemsie safely, and on time Sergeant Ambria made a phone call to Lieutenant Donavan back at the Algoria Army Base Head quarter.

Lieutenant Donovan has agreed to aid Dr. Xaviella and her team with getting the supplies to Chemsie.

One-week later Dr. Xaviella, Constable Caroline and Professor Cailynn arrived in the tiny village of Malvina in Chemsie. Once more all five Cousins were united as they work side by side for the betterment of humanity.

One particular morning Sergeant Ambria woke up with an adrenaline rush for excitement. After having breakfast, he had a brief meeting with his team. At the end of the meeting he pulled Santana aside and ask her if she would like to venture out by going for a test flight. Santana could not conceal her excitement as her eyes twinkles. Half an hour later they were good to go.

Sirens blaze signalling everyone to go underground to seek shelter as over head the war planes known as Avenger position to fire. A few minutes later bomb rain down on the city. Frantically the people scream as they seek cover. Several children were being caught in the rubbles as buildings came crashing down all around them. Men, women and children were being blown to pieces as the bombs fell. In the tunnels below people could be heard screaming franticly. They were filled with fear as they huddled together in the tunnels.

Ten minutes into their flight Sergeant Ambria's curiosity has caused him to change course and flew towards the no-fly zone bordering Chemsie and Am See. As he approaches the zone immediately a strange reading registered on his radar. Within seconds pictures started displaying on the screen. He was mortified as he looks at the pictures.

In an open wooded area was a group of about one hundred people being bundled together and surrounding them was a group of men dress like soldiers. He relates the scene to Santana whose breath caught in her throat, when she realized that the people were being massacre by the men in uniform. The engine of the F16 fighter jet was silent and so the people has no idea that they're being spied on.

Sergeant Ambria and Santana took several pictures of the massacre before heading back to their base in Chemsie. Sick to the stomach Santana climbed out the jet and hurry back to her station. She reported herself as being sick and took the rest of the day off. Before leaving for her apartment Sergeant Ambria let Santana sworn to secrecy never to discuss with anyone what they had discover earlier during their flight.

Santana swore then turn briskly on her heels and fled the camp as if she was being chase by a ghost. In the cool of the day Sergeant Ambria went back to the aircraft and remove the video from the plane, anger swirling through him as he walks back to his camp.

Each day Santana and Lieutenant Ambria perform their duties as though nothing happens. Deep down in their hearts they knew better but to speak of their findings to the rest of the group or to Lieutenant Donavan back at Headquarter would be adding fuel for the neighbouring countries to not only partake in the war, but placing himself as well as his crew in great danger. This secret lays heavy on both his and Santana's heart. Not once has Santana mentioned this to her sister Xaviella or to her Cousins.

Seven Months Later

Antwan Mavakura, leader of the Joachite Rebels was killed by one of Sergeant Ambria team member and two of his partners. Two weeks after the death of their leader the Joachite Rebels surrendered and equal rights and justice was given to the Wasabi Tribe. The women and children that were being taken hostages was returned to their village and was once more re-united with their families.

The Government has given a certain amount of money to the Melvina Community to rebuild their Schools, Clinics, their Synagogues and their stores. Now that the war has ended Santana along with Lieutenant Ambria and their group of Soldiers has returned to their station in Watta Dilly County.

Dr. Xaviella, Journalist Teanna, Constable Caroline and Professor Cailynn has also returned home from Chemsie. They were happy to return back to their families, Co-Workers and Friends safely, even though they were over exhausted.

The Cousins has decided to take some time off and rest before returning back to work.

After being away for so long, now that they've return the Cousins were looking forward to having some fun. Dr. Shaquille was over joy to see his Colleague again, but as soon as he realized how tired Dr. Xaviella was he encouraged her to take some time off and rest.

"I have everything under control." He assures her. Dr. Xaviella thank him and head out the door. On the drive home all she could think of was the haunting faces of the women and children back in Chemsie from shock and fear as looters raids the city night after night. She also remembers the smiles on the faces of the many mothers and elderly Ladies she has treated, but she will always carry the memory and the face of one particular mother.

A teenage girl with an infant son that has suffers severe dehydration.

No amount of money in the world would have given her the joy she felt when she was Given a case of bottle water and medicine for herself and her son who was being treated for three long days in hope of saving him. Dr. Xaviella was overwhelmed with joy knowing that her trip to Chemsie was not in vain. She felt totally satisfied knowing that she has given hope to others when all hope seems lost.

Back at the Algoria Army Head Quarter Lieutenant Donavan congratulates Sergeant Ambria and his team of Soldiers on a job well done in bringing down the Joachite Leader which led to the surrender of the Joachite Rebels group.

Sergeant Ambria and all the soldier's that went with him to Chemsie were all given a week off work, to spend with their families and friends.

"How wonderful it is to be home," said Teanna as she wonders around in her kitchen.

Opening the fridge, she reaches for a bottle of olives. She opens the bottle and pop two olives in her mouth. She chews slowly savouring the taste.

On the way home Caroline stop at her workplace at the 33 Police Division. She met officer John on her way in. He congratulates her for her bravery in going to Chemsie and giving of her time to help the less fortunate. She thanks him and went in search of her Boss Corporal Slitherton.

Corporal Slitherton didn't welcome Constable Carolynn with open arms but was rather upset that she has went away for such a long time.

"If you want to fire me, go ahead Corporal" But know this I Have chosen to stay away for a good cause. Let me assure you Corporal Slitherton that the people of the Malvina Village are far more appreciative than a lot of the officers I've worked with here

"What brought you to this conclusion Constable?"

"The simple fact that God has given me the opportunity to work with so many families in the Villages torn by the war and watch their faces lit up at the sight of a simple bottle of water, I saw the tears the many women have shed when being handed a package of personal feminine items.

"Do you know why Corporal Slitherton?"

'No Constable.'

'Because somebody took the time to show them they care.' Now if you have nothing more to say; I would like some more time off to rest as I'm exhausted.

Corporal Slitherton stares at Constable Caroline for some time before he said......

"Permission granted."

Constable Caroline thank him and walk out the door.

Professor Cailynn didn't know what to expect from the head of the school board. The Head Master confirms her trip giving her the ok to leave for Chemsie but they didn't knew that she would be gone for Seven long months.

Embracing herself for the un-expected she step into Principal O'Hara's office. Peering over her glasses Principal O'Hara wave to a chair telling her to sit down.

'Welcome Back Professor Cailynn!' and how did you find your experience in Chemsie?

'It was overwhelming, and allows me to appreciate my life here more.' Replied Professor Cailynn.

'How so?'

'One never knows the traumas the people living in a war torn country suffers until you experience it firsthand.' Continue Professor Cailyn.

'I see!' States Principal O'Hara.

'Will those victims ever truly heal?' Professor Cailyn asks Principal O'Hara.

"We can only pray and ask God to heal them Professor as we continue to give them our support in whatever way we can.'

Rising slowly Professor Cailyn place her hand over Principal O'Hara's right hand and ask her for a few weeks to recover from her trip and the heart wrenching things she has encounter during her stay in Chemsie.

Three Glorious weeks of endless fun

The Cousins' were all given three weeks off from their jobs to de-stress from their time being spend in Chemsie during the war and so they have decided to spend every day having fun by spending as much time together as they possible could before returning back to work.

Their first day out was spent going to Playdium where they went Go Cart Riding, Baseball batting and endless hours playing just about every game being set up inside of Playdium. The evening was still early and so they have decided to have something to eat After dinner they to the Theatre to watch the Avengers.

Twenty minutes into the film memories of their time in Chemsie came rushing back to them and so they got up exit that section of the Theatre and went in search of a film more exciting. They settled on watching The Inseparables. A film about the value of true friendship and sticking together no matter what.

This film very much compliments the characteristics as well as the friendship share between these Five Cousins. At the ending of the film the Cousins left the Theatre feeling much closer than they've been before. They call it a night and went to their separate homes.

The next day the weather was hotter than usual. A whopping 30 degrees It was a whopping 30 degree and so the Cousins has decided to spent the entire day swimming at Caroline's who have a big swimming pool in her backyard. They invited several family members as well as friends. They BBQ Chicken, Beef Kebobs and Grill fish while they sip on Margarita, Pina Colado and ice-cold Heineken Beer. This day was what introduces them back into the company of close relatives and friends after spending such heart wrenching time during the war for seven long months

How wonderful it feels to be surrounded by the people you love said Teanna to the rest of the Cousins as she pours herself a glass of ice cold water.

'I totally agree!' Replied Xaviella as she takes a bite off her chicken.

It wasn't always fun for the Cousins as from time to time they have all suffered some kind of break down from their horrific encounter during their stay in Chemsie. The one who suffers most was Santana. Night after night she had nightmares as her mind replays the scene of the massacre of about a hundred civilians she and Sergeant Ambria has witnessed while flying in the no-fly zone. They have come across this massacre by accident.

Now her nightmares are becoming much worse. She enjoyed spending time and having fun with her Cousins whom one by one began noticing the signs of her fatigue and discomfort as well as the many complaint she made to them in regards to her pounding headache.

One morning after waking up from a terrible night Santana wrote— My mind is consumed with the voices in my head. When the voices began to speak my mind is no longer my own as the voices hold me in a trance like grip until it has decided to release me. Everywhere I look I see people dying, I hear a tumult of children crying as the sound of guns and bombs echoes everywhere.

My mind reels my eyes palpitate as my body breaks out in sweat and convulse as thou I'm in a Fitz. The voices taunt me as the images of the people haunts me. Closing my eyes I hang my head as I wrapped my arms around my body and curled up on the floor.

'Oh God when will these voices and images release me, and stop setting fire to my mind?'

O God I beg you please let it stop please let these nightmares stop haunting me.

Nervously I pull at my hair as though I'm going insane while I just lay there and scream.

My mind mess up I become confused as I'm caught between reality and a dream.

'Stop!' O God please let it stop I can't take it anymore I scream. My voice becomes a whisper as I rock back and forth. Suddenly all become clear and calm again as the voices and images fades away and no longer haunts me, thus giving my mind back to me once more. I dread the night in fear of falling asleep as my nightmares will begin all over again.

Dr. Xaviella has given her a complete check and after hours of probing Santana has related the incident to her, but not before letting Dr. Xaviella vowed never to discuss or speak of it with the rest of the Cousins or anyone else as a matter of fact.

Xaviella being not just a doctor but her sister has encouraged her to see a psychiatrist before returning back to work. At first Santana was sceptic about seeing a psychiatrist but has taken the plunge when her nightmares were now becoming too much for her to bear. She then schedules an appointment with Dr. LaBelle, whom has gotten her back on track after their seventh session.

Ridding her conscience of what she has seen to Dr. LaBelle has caused Santana's nightmares to cease thus allowing her to function as her old self again. Three times during their three weeks' vacation the Cousins were picked up by Limousine to several function. The first time was for a night out on the town in the heart of the city where they dine at the Xacole Restaurant, one of the city's finest.

The second time was to the Air Canada Centre where they watch a playoff of the Toronto Raptors against the New York Braves, and the third time was to the Roy Thompson Hall Theatre where they watch the performance of the Million Dollar Quartet. Other days were spent going to the nail salon, to the spa, shopping and working around the house.

Two Years Later

Sergeant Ambria has found the courage to reveal his findings of the massacre when he enters the no-fly zone bordering Chemsie and Am See to Lieutenant Donavon and Colonel Rudolph DeBourge. They were furious after watching the video.

Both Lieutenant Donavon and Colonel DeBourge has setup a secret meeting with the Ambassador of the UN Mr. Deon Cobart to discuss the possibility of sending some of their soldiers along with secret agents of the UN to investigate the area of the no-fly zone between Chemsie and Am See to learn if it's really Soldiers or Rebels pretending to be Soldiers that are carrying out such savage act.

Five months into the investigation another war broke out between Am See and the Chiacah Tribe of their neighbouring country Gigota. When one of Am See's fighter jet was shot down by their own arm force who has mistaken the jet for one of the Chiacah Rebels Aircraft, this was not taken very well by the Am See's Government. He wants revenge.

Once again Sergeant Ambria and his Team were sent to Am See for peace keeping.

Commander Santana was replaced by Colonel David Hues, who was rather excited to venture on this mission. Commander Santana spent most of her time at the Algoria Head Quarter working with Lieutenant Donavon, Colonel Rudolph DeBourge and the UN Ambassador Mr. Deon Cobert, they work valiantly in locating and defeating the group responsible for the grave massacre which has taken place two years prior.

The Chiacah Rebels rains bomb on the city with very little regards for the innocent men, women and children that inhabits the city. Sergeant Ambria felt fear for the first time since arriving with his crew. He's schedule to fly out over Am See to see how much damage is being inflicted on the city. Sadly, his jet was shot down by the Chiacah rebels.

Upon being captured Sergeant Ambria was being held in a dark room without food or water. In the middle of the night pain ripped through his body, he thought he was going to die. As his life flashed before him he began to pray....

Open up to me the gate of freedom that I may enter through them O lord, and I shall give thanks to the Lord for this is the day that you have made me to be captured by the Enemies, but I'm asking you dear God not to let them over power me. Please make a way of escape for me that I will return back to my friends, the members of my crew and to my family.

You are my God and I give thanks to you, you are my God and I extol you. Your right hand is exalted O Lord, your right hand does valiantly; therefore I shall live and not die.

O God please rescue my soul from death, my eyes from tears, and my feet from stumbling. Please preserve my life from my enemies.

In my dark hour when I thought I wouldn't make it, when I thought my enemies would convocated me, please shine light in the heart of my enemies and allow them to freely and voluntarily save me.

Though they have shot me down like a prey, I have given my service to deliver the Poor, and the Orphans who are paying the price daily with their lives, for the greed of those blood thirsty bastards fighting not for the good of the people but for selfish gains and power to satisfy their lust to control the less fortunate. I have come here God not for war but to the peace. If you are listening please allow me to return back home to my family and friends. Don't let me die here. Sergeant Ambria has no idea as to when he passed out.

Three days later Sergeant Ambria woke up in a bunker surrounded by computers and other communication devices. Looking around him he wanted to know what had happen.

There was no one around. Pain ripped through him as his head throbbed. The door to the bunker was closed, there was no escaping for him, he was trapped.

Cautiously he looks around him. He was mortified when his eyes located a casket looking box in one corner of the room with several wires attached to it. Getting up slowly he walked over to it. Inside was the body of a beautiful young woman who appears to be dead. Looking closely Sergeant Ambria realize that the woman wasn't dead. She's alive even though she's being submerged in liquid.

"Could it be that the Chiacah Rebels is using her for experiment?" He wonders. For years scientists have been working tirelessly in trying to find a way in which to clone humans. After years of research and hard work in genetic decoding they were successful in cloning a sheep in England.

Sergeant Ambria looks around the room once more then wandered back over to the strange looking capsule. Cautiously he open the lid. He was fascinated with the beautiful figure lying inside. It has been a while since he has seen such beauty, such perfection.

For Lieutenant Ambria time stood still as he drools over the woman lying there in the strange looking liquid as though she has been frozen in time with the techniques of science and technology. For a brief moment he wandered back to the computers and tried turning them on. His top priority is to find a way out of the bunker and find a way to get back to his crew. With no one around other than the figure lying in the capsule Sergeant Ambria was desperate to get word back to his camp or to his Headquarter in Algoria.

Beside one of the computer sits a bottle of whisky. Sergeant Ambria quickly open the bottle and pour some in his mouth in hopes of numbing the pain scourging through his body. Within seconds he heard one of the computers in the far corner of the room making a strange noise. Being caught off guard he was shock to see the woman in the casket looking capsule raised her hands and started pushing on the lid of the capsule.

As she does this a warning signal went off somewhere in the building. Noise could be heard coming from the outside as a man shout orders. Sergeant Ambria crouch in a corner and pretend to be asleep when he heard the door to the room opening. A tall man with heavy built and ice blue eyes stalk into the room and rush towards the capsule.

Paying no attention to Sergeant Ambria the man busied himself with the woman in the capsule. Opening the lid, the man reached down and yanks the woman up out of the water looking liquid. She gasps for air as she sat up.

"So Gina are you ready to talk now?' asked the man in a course voice.

'Never!' replied the woman.

He was a about to push her back down in the liquid when Sergeant Ambria sprang into action. He got up, rushed over to the man and wrestles him to the ground. They battle each other for some time. Ignoring his pain, Sergeant Ambria fought and fought. He was determined to get out of this place where he was being held against his will.

The young woman steps out of the capsule, ripped the wires from her hands and head. Feebly she helps Sergeant Ambria fought the man that wandered into the room. Finally gaining the upper hand and laying hold of the man's gun Sergeant Ambria shot the man he sees as his enemy, took his card undress him and quickly change into his clothes and walk out the room camouflage as one of his capturer with the lovely Gina following close beside him.

Within minutes Sergeant Ambria and Gina made it to a nearby wood where they spent the night in hiding. Sergeant Ambria learnt that Gina's envoy was ambushed by the Chiacah Rebels two weeks prior. She knew nothing of the rest of her crew as she was being hold for question and when she refused to talk she was placed into the casket looking capsule filled with some kind of strange liquid that keeps her alive in a sleep state like the fetus within a mother's womb.

Together Gina and Sergeant Ambria travel for a week taking care of each other as they tried to survive on berries during the day while scouting their surroundings as to which way will lead them back to the neighbouring village of Am See. The Chaicah Rebels search endlessly for the both of them but were unable to find them as they made their way deeper and deeper into the woods.

Commander Santana follows the news hourly in fear for the safety of his best friend Sergeant Ambria and his Team in Gigota and for her

Cousin Teanna. At precisely 16:00 hour on Wednesday the 9th day of January time stood still for Commander Santana when she turns on the TV just in time to hear Reporter Teanna delivers the news. She learnt that Sergeant Ambria's aircraft went missing a week and some days and that Sergeant Ambria didn't make it back to his base and is feared as being dead.

'God damn it!' Teanna I hope that statement was a miss understanding, Santana whispers as she forces herself to breathe. Commander Santana quickly turn off the TV and went in search of Lieutenant Donovan. She saw him walking towards a group of soldiers with a stock of paper in his hand. Commander Santana started running as she call.

'Lieutenant!' May I have a word with you please, Sir.

'Is everything ok Commander?'

'No Sir!'

'Don't just stand there; tell me what's bothering you Commander.'

Santana pause for a brief moment before she speaks.

'I just saw it on the news Sir, that Sergeant Ambria's aircraft didn't make it back to his base after he went flying some days ago Sir.'

'Are you sure of this Commander?'

'Yes Sir!' that's what my Cousin that's covering the news reported Sir.'

'Thank you, Commander.' I'll get on top of this news immediately. Headquarter know nothing of this.

'You're welcome Sir!'

Immediately Lieutenant Donovan turn around and walk briskly back to his office.

Commander Santana prays a prayer for Sergeant Ambria and force herself to believe that Teanna was wrong. Lieutenant Donovan spend three hours on the phone handling calls to the base of Sergeant Ambria in Gigota trying desperately to figure out what went wrong with Sergeant's Ambria and his aircraft. He was mortified when that which Commander Santana had related to him earlier on Sergeant Ambria was confirmed.

'He was the best damn Pilot of the group that's there,' said Lieutenant

Donovan angrily as he slams his fist on his desk. "Why were we not informed of this before now?"

As not to upset Commander Santana with his findings that, that which she has related to him is true Lieutenant Donovan busied himself with the head of the UN Commissioner discussing the details on how to search and find the secret base of the Chiacah Rebels and bringing them to justice.

Panic and concern gripped Sergeant Ambria's team members since the day his plane didn't made it back to their base. The day his aircraft fail to return they carried out a search of their own trying to locate the Sergeant but was un successful in their search. It's been a week and two days since Sergeant Ambria and his plane went missing. Wing commander Castel Hues and four other soldiers sets out on a search for the missing Sergeant. They search way into the evening but find nothing.

"Tomorrow we search again he said as he walks back to his tent.

Woe unto us, for the day declines, for the shadows of the evening lengthen; arise and let us attack by night. Cast up a siege against Am See, Violence and destruction are heard in her streets.

'Come let us arise and go and find our fallen comrade!' Said wing commander Hues to his team upon waking up the next day. Five Officers agreed to go into the City with him.

They drove to a little Village called Dedam. They were waiting at a stop light. The light turn green and they drove off with no particular route in mind. About seventy metres in front of them a little boy around the age of three rolled a ball into the street and began chasing after it. Colonel Hues slammed his foot on the brake and slow his speed in order not to hit the child.

He had no idea as to where the child came from or what was happening, but he senses that something was desperately wrong. As the jeep slowed out of nowhere came a group of men with their faces painted all black and their bodies covered in bushes and began firing at them from every side. When he looks for the child, he was nowhere in sight.

Wing Commander Hues and two other soldiers scream and shout as they return the fire. In less than ten minutes three of his officers were dead. He reached for the radio and was immediately shot in the arm. He whelps from the pain. Frantically he radios back to the base in Gigota.

'Code Red!' This is Wing Commander Hues; my men and I have been ambushed in the village of Dedam.

'Is everyone safe Sir?' Ask the voice on the other end of the radio.

'No Sir!' Three of my men are dead, another near death and I'm shot send back up he shout.

'Help is on the way Sir.

'Thank you Sir'

Wing Commander Hues was about to answer when he and the other remaining officer were both shot. Immediately the other soldier died from a shot to the head. Colonel Hues pressed the gas as hard as he could in hope of getting to safety. Paying little attention to the blood he's losing and the dead bodies around him, Wing Commander Hues drove and drove. When it was safe he stopped on a lonely and deserted road. He pulled over to the side.

He jumped out of the jeep and scream.

'Jesus Christ this is frigging insane:' That frigging little bastard was used as a trap to slow us down.'

He kicks the wheel of the jeep and holds his head. Falling to his knees he said I should have killed the son of a bitch. 'Now all my men are dead, he cried.

Half an hour later Wing Commander Hues was picked up by Officer Andre Sullivan and the Arm force Physician Dr. Octavia Adair who attends to his wounds. They were accompanied by another group of soldiers who took the wing Commander and the bodies of his men back to their camp. Chaplain Dwight Johnson, Corporal Larry Williams, General Kennard Campbell and Pilot Kenny McLaren has fought many battles. Together they were swifter than eagles, stronger than lions. In life they were inseparable and in death they were not divided.

Back at the base tension rise as they waited for news on Sergeant Ambria and for the envoy that went to rescue wing Commander Hues and his men and their safe return. At the camp soldiers watched both in shock and relief when Officer Sullivan's jeep was spotted rolling in the driveway of the camp. A group of Soldiers ran out to meet them.

Soldiers watched in harrow as the bloody bodies were un load from the jeep. They embraced each other and cry.

It's been now two and a half weeks since Sergeant Ambria went missing. They were about to rule out Sergeant Ambria as dead, when suddenly he showed up with the Lovely Gina. They were both looking pale, tired, and over exhausted. Shouts rang out throughout the camp as everyone welcome them. Sergeant Ambria and Gina wasted no time telling the rest of the soldiers about what has happen to them and how they manage to escape.

Gina was given food and clothing by Abigail a medical assistant of Sergeant Ambria's team who has spent two days monitoring both Gina and Sergeant Ambria whom were under her medical supervision. Gina spent five days with Sergeant Ambria and his team who took it upon themselves to return her to the Am See Army headquarter back to her team safe and secure.

Sergeant Ambria and his team members were all given a medal of Honor by Colonel Tiam Shi Agachi head of the Am See Arm Force for their bravery and a job well done in returning Officer Gina safely and for bringing down the Chaicah Rebels by exposing them and bringing them to justice.

The battle between Am Sea and the Chaicah Tribe of Gigota was short lived as the UN has gotten a break through on the story they were working on and brought a group of Soldiers who were working secretly with the Am Sea Government in bringing the Chiacah Rebels to justice. All the neighbouring Countries as well as their Leaders were in shock when the story leaks out. It was a humiliating blow to the president of Gigota and the rest of his Political party.

Two and a half months later the war has ended. This time around it was more heart wrenching for Lieutenant Ambria than the time he has spent in Chemsie, as he has lost eight of his Soldiers to the Chiacah Rebels when their envoy was being ambushed in the City of Goah. He watched in silence as the caskets carrying their bodies were being loaded on a C-12F Cargo plane.

Sergeant Ambria has fought many battles, and many times he has patrol the streets in honour of keeping the peace but this particular war has left him extremely cold and numb. Before climbing aboard the air craft he whispers a prayer for his fallen Comrades and their families they have left behind; and will now be morning them when they return to their country. Why God has chosen to spare his life he does not know but one thing is for certain, He is thankful to be alive. It makes him feel proud of all his Partners who have lost their lives fighting for a just cause. He might not be able to heal all the broken hearted, but this he knows that he along with each soldier that has lost their lives has labour and toil endlessly for the sake of others to make the world a safer and a much better place for those that are left behind.

Two of Constable Carolline's Officers was gunned down as well in battle and died in the line of duty at a HSBC Bank on Highway 10 and Conestoga Drive which was robbed by three armed men. It was no easy task for her to relate the sad news to Officer Mallich Occonor, and Officer Adear LeFemme's family. She didn't hesitate in telling them of the Officer's bravery, as well as how much they're loved and being missed by all.

Three Weeks later

Corporal Rowshane Campanni's Funeral

A procession of Soldiers marched behind the Hurst carrying the body of Officer Roshane Campanni's body from St. Lutheran's church on Shangai Avenue, a three-Mile-long walk to the cemetery at the corner of Wilkinson and Guthard Lane. Both sides of the street were lined with Citizens who has made it their duty to come out and show their support and respect to the family of the fallen soldier's families and friends, along with hundreds of Soldiers stand attentively as the Hurst enters the Cemetery. Within minutes the casket was wheeled to the side of the grave. Heart thumping and palms sweating Commander Santana and Sergeant Ambria watched unblinkingly as Lieutenant Donovan gave orders to the Soldiers commanding them to fold the Canadian Flag covering the casket which was then handed to Commander Santana, who in turn present it to Corporal Rowshane's wife and family.

'Attention!' Shout the Officer in charge of the gun Salute.

Commander Santana and Sergeant Ambria comfort each other with their eyes as more commands rang out.

'Fire'

The sound of Shots echoes everywhere as each weapon barks out sounds of Respect for the fallen Soldier. Before leaving the Cemetery, Commander Santana gave a card expressing her condolences along with her telephone number to Corporal Rowshane's wife, gave her a hug and told her to call her should she needed someone to talk to.

Sergeant Ambria has kept in touch with Gina Pascalie after returning back to Canada after the war. Gina has agreed to visit him. They fell in love and nine months they got married. The many years of war has left its scars on Sergeant Ambria's Heart, thus making it difficult for him to function without living the shady nightmares of his pass. He began drinking due to his depression. He did a fine job in hiding both his depression and his drinking from his wife Gina. One night he was out with a couple of his friends eating and drinking in a bar. Savouring the taste of his steak Sergeant Ambria felt a fire burning deep in his chess from his Irish whisky. Each tingling sensation was mix with desire for his beautiful wife Gina.

Slowly he chew on his steak, each bite filled with passionate desire and longing. In his mind eyes he sees his wife smiling seductively at him as she bares her left shoulder; her skin glowing making him hot inside. Sergeant Ambria gulped down his last shot of whisky and shook himself. It was during this time he has confided in his closest friend Mitch that he's seriously thinking of committing suicide as his nightmares along with his stress is getting too much for him to bear.

'And what of your wife?' ask Mitch. You can't bring her here, marry her and now wanted to flunk out on her Ambria. This doesn't make sense.

'At least she doesn't have to worry about war anymore as she's now living in a safe and peaceful Country;' Tsked Sergeant Ambria.

'Ha— have you ever taken the time to reminisce on the time your plane got shot down by the Chaicah Rebels and how they could have killed you when they captured you? Ask Sam.

'There's not a day goes by and I haven't thought about it' replied Sergeant Ambria.

'Then I suggest you get this bull shit idea of killing yourself out of your head.'

They had another round of beer then call it a night. Pushing his chair back almost knocking it to the ground Sergeant Ambria walks out the bar. The ride home was a long one. As Sergeant Ambria drove he allows himself to reflect back on the many countries he has been to for peace keeping. The many people that has died around him and the many times he has escape death. Sadden he turns on the radio. Elvis Presley song love me tender echoes through the speakers.

His mind drifts back to the time he woke up in the bunker and saw the most beautiful woman he has ever seen laying in the casket looking capsule. How he wanted her even though at the time he knew not if she was dead or alive. Now that very woman is his wife. What gives him the right to be thinking such hideous thoughts of wanting to kill himself?

If the good Lord wanted him dead he would have killed him a long time ago during the many encounters he had in the line of duty. Life with Gina isn't that bad? After all he's the one that caused her to be reacting the way she does lately.

His constant nightmares have caused him to become overly stressed and traumatized, and instead of seeking help or discussing them with his wife he does everything in his power to shut her out. Sergeant Ambria pulled up in his driveway and sat in the car for a while before coming out. Few minutes later he staggers to the front door put his key into the lock then staggers inside.

Gina was sitting in the living room in the dark waiting for her husband to come home.

Sergeant Ambria shriek when he turns on the light and sees her there.

'What are you doing down here sitting down in the dark?'

'I was waiting for you. I was worried when I didn't hear you come in.'

'Well, as you can see I'm here now.' he drawled as he staggers towards her.

The smell of alcohol waft towards Gina. Angrily she got up and was up into her husband's face with just two steps

'You know how much I hate the smell of alcohol she hissed' Are you drunk because you no longer wanted to be with me?'

'No my love, you know how much I love you. That's why I marry you.'

'Then why are you acting so strange for the last three months?'

'It breaks my heart to see that your lack of love for me has blind you my husband.'

'You of all people should understand the stress war can leave a soldier, my dear wife.'

'Believe me Sergeant I understand more than you'll ever know,' however, it would make me happier if you stop shutting me out the way you do.' You have taken me from a war torn country and have brought me here, where for the first time, for as long as I can

Remember I found peace. "Do you know what it's like afraid to fall asleep at night because you are afraid you might not live to see the next morning?" She asks

"Yes, honey I do.".

You and your men has become a ruler over the Chaicah Rebels and has brought them low before the law of Justice. For many years other tried and failed but you and your men succeed. She continues.

Pulling Gina into his arms Sergeant Ambria apologizes to her, take her by the hand and led her upstairs to bed. They made love way into the early morn for the first time in three months. The next morning Sergeant Ambria awoke with a terrible headache from his hangover, he phones Lieutenant Donovan and told him he's in need of some time off to spend with his wife.

Conclusion

Six Months Later

One bleak afternoon Sergeant Ambria went to the back of the house and find himself a piece of rope and made his way hurriedly back to the kitchen. He's over stressed from his Job and his never-ending nightmares. His wife Gina has become distance after failing time and time again in her attempts to help him, and so now he sees suicide as the only way out as his wife offers him very little hope. Now all she does is whine and complain on a daily basis.

There're so many things Sergeant Ambria wanted to share with his wife Gina. Each time he approaches her she withdrew into herself and said nothing. Sergeant Ambria couldn't cope with being ignored by Gina any longer. Failing in his attempt to speak to her one evening after dinner, he made his way to the shed at the back of the house while rehearsing in his mind how to carry out his plan.

Entering the shed he picked up the rope made a noose and tied it to a beam in the roof.

He was about to place the noose around his neck when he heard footsteps approaching.

He walks over to the small window of the shed and look outside. He sees no one, but he sense that someone was there.

'Ambria!' Call Gina.

Panic seized Ambria upon hearing his wife calling his name. His heart began pounding as he look through the window once more in silence.

'Ambria!' Are you there? Gina called once more. This time a bit louder.

Sergeant Ambria knocks over a ladder in his haste to go and secure the lock of the door to the shed. Gina heard the noise and rushes towards the shed and began pounding on the door. After several minutes of pleading with her husband; Sergeant Ambria opened the door. Looking inside Gina shine a light inside and saw the rope with the noose tied to the ledge. She panics and rushed towards him

'What's this?' she asked angrily.

Sergeant Ambria look passed her in grave silence.

Beating his chess with her fist Gina started crying.

'Why? Why?' was all she managed to ask.

Tears welled up in her husband eyes as gentle he pulled her into his arms.

"If you have nothing else to live for whispers Gina, please live for our child."

Hearing this Sergeant Ambria cry like a baby as he let his memory drift back to that night in the dark room where he was being locked up in the bunker or the basement, wherever it was when his plane was shot down in Am See, and the prayer he has prayed to God when he thought he wouldn't' make it out alive.

'You are.....You are pregnant? He asks his wife in a hoarse voice.

'Yes, my love.' Exactly two and a half months.

'O God please forgive me, he repeats over and over.'

Sergeant Ambria kissed his wife and apologizes to her. Cutting the rope from the beam he head back to the house; Gina holding on to his arms.

Two and a half years later

They had dinner and talk for hours. With Gina's help and support her husband was helped by a Psychiatrist. Sergeant Ambria had agreed and sign up with Dr. Laura Hopkins physiatrist who has helped several Soldiers at Algoria Army Base. After six months of intense therapy he was well again.

Gina has given birth to her second child a beautiful daughter who is now eight months old. Her relationship with her husband has taken on a whole new life of its own.

Sergeant Ambria no longer suffers from nightmares or any past war phobias.

Giving birth to their first son has mend the fences and the bridges that were once broken between her and her husband. Now they're happy and living a normal family life. On weekends when her husband comes home he spent most of his time recruiting his young son Johnny, teaching him about life in the army. Sergeant Ambria and Gina hope that when Johnny grows up and become a man he too would follow in their footsteps and join the Army.

From time to time Sergeant Ambria and his wife, their two years old son Johnny and their eight months old daughter Belinda visit his best friend and former flying partner Commander Santana and her family. He'll never forget the first time he met her how bossy and pushy she was. At first, he taught she was stuck up then he learns that she is a kind and gentle soul, she only relates that tough attitude to prove to the guys that not because she is a woman they think she is an easy target to be pushed around.

Not only is Sergeant Ambria having the time of his life recruiting young soldiers in the Army he looks forward on a weekly basis to going home and spending leisure time on the weekends with his wonderful wife and kids

As the sun rose over the horizon Commander Santana gets ready to recruit a group of Soldiers. She pours herself a cup of coffee. Sitting at the table she read through the names of the soldiers she'll be recruiting. She recognized one of the names on the list.

Antoine Sebalski. He was a student at the Metatron University where she attends school.

Interesting she said to herself. Finishing her coffee she picked up her list and head out the door.

The group of young recruits busied themselves exercising while waiting for Commander Santana. As she approach they watch with great interest.

'Good morning boys!'

'Good morning Commander.'

Officer Sebalski watches her curiously as he tries to remember where he has seen Commander Santana before.

"Permission to ask a question Commander." He said to Santana.

'And what would you like to know soldier?'

'Your face as well as your name looks and sounds familiar to me'

'What's your question Sebalski?'

'Were you a student at the Metatron University? He asks.

Commander Santana raised a brow and watches him warily. 'I could ask the same question of you Sebalski.

'I did attend Metraton University!' He replied.

'Then let me say that I too have attend Metraton University several years ago.

"Did I answer your question solder?'

'Yes Commander' you did'

Removing the cover from her pen Commander Santana went through her list making sure all her recruited were present. This being done she gave the orders. An hour into training a young soldier named Trevor violated the rules and was placed in confinement. General Kenrick and Commander Santana interrogate him.

'What makes you think you're more special than everyone here?' General Kenrick asks him.

Trevor look pass him in silence. Commander Santana walks over to soldier and place her mouth close his left ear.

'When your superior speaks to you, you answer. You hear me soldier?' Now answer the question or I shall use a greater force against you.'

"I need one hundred push ups, followed by one hundred jumping jacks she informed them.

Immediately the soldiers get down and start exercising. Commander Santana spent four hours drilling her soldiers before releasing them and sending them back to the camp.

Constable Caroline put on her lipstick, pick up her gun and place it in its holder.

Picking up her car keys she heads out the door. She's attending a Sermon being held in honour of Officer Sean Demuir who is being promoted to Chief of the officers. She Was playing a reggae cd. A song addressing Jamaican's living in foreign counties not to send guns to the Island but rather food computers, books and medicine for the less fortunate children living on the Island.

A group of youngsters pulled up beside her in a escalade, the driver look over at her and smile. She smiles back.

'Nice music officer!' He said.

'Yes!'

'Respect to you officer!' said the young man before driving off.

Santana served another three years in the Arm Force after returning from the battle in Chemsie after which she has resigned and went on to pursue her career as a Model once more. She Model for S Models and one of Germany's top shoe Designer David Dudek heel the world in Munich Germany where she now lives with her Fiancé while enjoying a wonderful relationship with her daughter Kyara, and her Sisters: Dr. Xaviella and Steffi, her brother Jakob as well as her friends. Her Maserati is her prize possession and she enjoys picnics in the park and traveling the world.

Teanna has given up her job as a Reporter for the KGB News Station a year after reporting the war on Gigota and Chemsie and has moved from Canada to Buffalo where she is working as a Wildlife Biologist saving the lives of her furry friends. She enjoys putting down the roof of her Tesla as she drives from city to city. She is engaged to a Drop Dead Gorgeous Scuba Diving Instructor and enjoys diving with her Fiancé off the coast of Mexico with the Dolphins.

Constable Caroline is still an officer of the 33 Division Police Force where she is now Head of the Forensic Squat Team. She's enjoying every minute of her job putting all the bad guys were they belong...behind bars. She is married to a wonderful Criminal Lawyer and have one daughter. When she's not chasing villains she enjoys cruising downtown Toronto with her husband in her Porsche. They are living in Ontario.

Professor Cailyn still Teaches at the Dubrovnik University where she is now Dean of the University. She has joined with Dr. Xaviella who is the founder of the Wasabi Charity which offers help to the women and children of the Melvida village in Chemsie and neighbouring cities.

She is living in Mississauga, Ontario with her boyfriend who is also a teacher at the University and their two Dogs and three Cats. She Drives a Ferrari

Dr. Xaviella has migrated back to Germany where she has opened her own Medical Clinic and has written several books on her experience in Chemsie as well as several medical books. She is also the founder of the Wijesekera Wasabi Charity which is gear to provide free medical care and education for the Wasabi Tribes in Chemsie and other tribes in the surrounding villages that are in need of care. All the Cousins are members and dedicated supporters of this Charity. She is married to a wonderful Architecture Engineer and is living in Munich with her husband and their son. She enjoys driving her Bugatti on the Autobahn.

The Cousins has made it their duties to visit each other twice per year, once being spent in a different country or city as they visit each other to catch up on the adventures going on in their lives. Most important of all; to spend quality time with each other as close family and friends. No matter where their adventure or their Careers has taken them the Cousins will forever be In-Separable.

The End

About the Author

Gloreen Hephizibah Burke mother of two beautiful daughters and two lovely grandchildren Kyara and Eljero has a BA in Law and is also the Author of Mother Nature Dear, The Magic Cookies, The girl who dreamt she was a Princess, Stranger in the Dark and several other Romance Novels. She lives in Ontario Canada with her family.

Printed in the United States
By Bookmasters